D1415507

the
meter
is

the
meter
is

By Jerolyn Ann Nentl

Library of Congress Catalog Card Number: 76-24200. International Standard Book Number: 0-913940-45-3.

Design - Doris Woods and Randal M. Heise

There is much discussion regarding the spelling of meter and liter. Often you will see these words spelled metre and litre. The -re spellings came from the French language, the language in which the metric system was developed. The United States seems to prefer the -er spellings.

Special Thanks to:

Dr. Mary Kahrs - Professor of Education at Mankato
                State University, Mankato, Minnesota

Mr. David L. Dye - Mathematics Consultant, St. Paul, Minnesota

PHOTO CREDITS

Mark Ahlstrom, Media House

R.M. Heise - Art Director.

the
meter
is

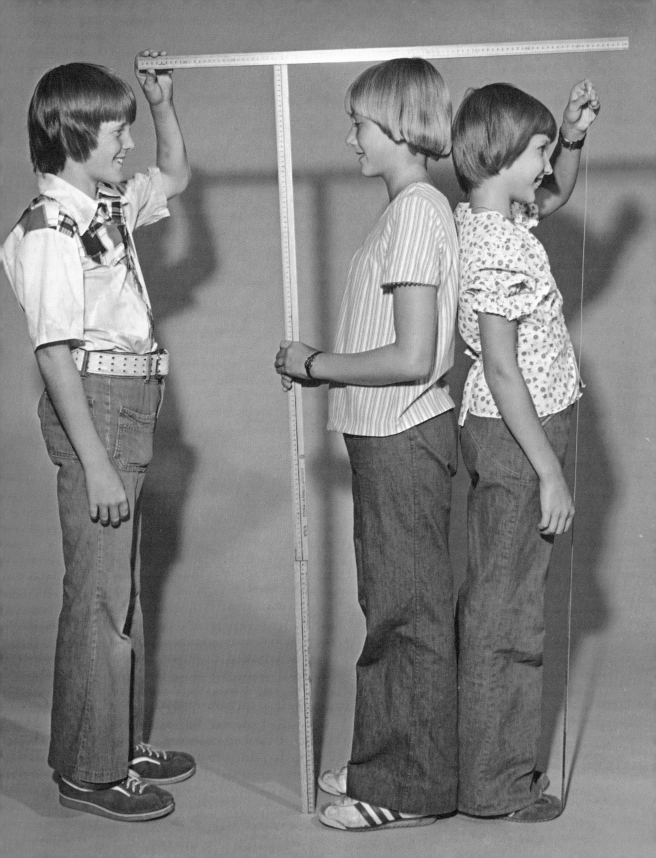

Do you remember the last time you measured yourself to find out how tall you were?

Perhaps it was when you went to the doctor and he asked you to stand on a large scale. He weighed you and slid a piece of flat metal down a pole until it touched the top of your head. Then he read the measurement markings on the pole to see how tall you were.

Or maybe you stood with your back against a wall and your brother or sister or a friend made a pencil mark on the wall at the top of your head. Then you measured from the floor to the pencil mark. Or did you simply borrow your mother's tape measure and stand on one end and stretch it above your head?

The school nurse may have had you stand in front of a door that held a brightly colored chart with measurement markings on it. Then she put her finger at the spot on the chart at the top of your head and told you how tall you were.

No matter how you did it, you probably measured the distance in feet or inches. You used a ruler marked to show 12 inches or one foot or a larger yardstick marked to show 36 inches or three feet.

With the metric system you will not be using inches, or feet, or yards anymore. You will using a

METER STICK

The meter stick looks almost like a yard stick. It is just a little bit longer than a yard stick. But the markings on it are much different. It is marked in

DECIMETERS

CENTIMETERS

MILLIMETERS

When you first see the words decimeter, centimeter and millimeter, they may look long and hard to pronounce and remember. They are really very simple words and very easy to use.

The basic unit of length in the metric system is the

METER

Scientists have agreed that a meter is "1 650 763.73 wavelengths of the orange-red light of the isotope krypton-86, measured in a vacuum." When the metric system was first planned, mathematicians determined that the meter was 1/10-millionth of the distance from the North Pole to the Equator.

These are important for the scientists and mathematicians to know, but they are not important kinds of definitions for students to remember. It is only important to know that scientists and mathematicians have worked hard to make the length of the meter so accurate that it is always the same, no matter where you are.

A meter is the same length in the United States as it is in Russia. Different governments cannot change how long 1 650 763.73 wavelengths of that orange-red light measure, or how far it is from the North Pole to the Equator.

A meter is the same length high on a mountaintop as it is in a submarine deep in the ocean. It is not affected by altitude. It is the same length in the hot jungles of South America as it is in the freezing cold of the Arctic Circle. It is not affected by temperature or the weather.

The meter can be divided into 10 DECIMETERS.

This is a DECIMETER.

You can make a meter stick to measure things by marking 10 of these lengths on a piece of paper or cardboard or a board or a stick.

Each decimeter is divided into 10 CENTIMETERS, so there are 100 centimeters in a meter.

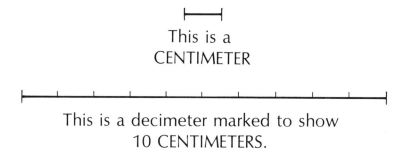

This is a
CENTIMETER

This is a decimeter marked to show
10 CENTIMETERS.

Now you can mark the centimeters on your meter stick.

And each centimeter is divided into 10 MILLIMETERS, so there are 100 millimeters in a decimeter and 1000 millimeters in a meter.

⊦

This is a
MILLIMETER

⊢⊔⊔⊔⊔⊔⊣

This is a centimeter marked
to show 10 MILLIMETERS.

You probably won't want to mark all 1000 millimeters on your meter stick, but it would help you measure very little things if you divided 1 or 2 centimeters on your stick into millimeters.

There is a very easy way to remember all of this.

Look back at each of the three new words: DECIMETER, CENTIMETER and MILLIMETER. You can see that each word is made up of the word "meter" and a prefix. Do you remember that a prefix is a syllable or a group of syllables added to the beginning of a word to make a new word?

In decimeter the prefix is DECI. In centimeter it is CENTI. In millimeter is it MILLI.

DECImeter.

CENTImeter.

MILLImeter.

There is a very good reason for making up the words this way. The prefixes are from the Latin language and refer to the sizes of things.

DECI means 1/10
CENTI means 1/100
MILLI means 1/1000

And you will remember that there are

10 DECImeters in a meter.

100 CENTImeters in a meter.

1000 MILLImeters in a meter.

With the millimeter, centimeter, and decimeter units of measurement, you can measure the lengths of small things.

You can measure things like:

the doorway in the doghouse you and your friend are building, to make sure your dog will fit.

the material for the pair of pants you are sewing, to make sure they are long enough.

the corn in your garden, to see how tall it is growing.

For bigger things, there are three other units of measurement to learn: DEKAMETER, HECTOMETER and KILOMETER. They are also very simple to remember and easy to use once you understand what they mean. They are made up of the word "meter" plus prefixes from the Greek language that refer to size.

DEKA means 10.

HECTO means 100.

KILO means 1000.

To measure larger things you must remember.

1 DEKAMETER equals 10 meters.

1 HECTOMETER equals 100 meters.

1 KILOMETER equals 1000 meters.

So there are seven new words to learn if you want to measure length in the metric system: MILLIMETER, CENTIMETER, DECIMETER, METER, DEKAMETER, HEC-TOMETER and KILOMETER.

The

METER

is the basic unit of measurement.

To measure small things you will use: decimeter, centimeter or millimeter.

DECIMETER equals 1/10 of a meter.
There are 10 decimeters in a meter.

CENTIMETER equals 1/100 of a meter.
There are 100 centimeters in a meter.

MILLIMETER equals 1/1000 of a meter.
There are 1000 millimeters in a meter.

To measure large things you will use: dekameter, hectometer and kilometer.

DEKAMETER equals 10 meters.

HECTOMETER equals 100 meters.

KILOMETER equals 1000 meters.

Of these seven new units of measurement, you probably will only use four of them very often: METER, CENTIMETER, MILLIMETER and KILOMETER.

The KILOMETER is the unit of distance for very long distances, like the distance between two cities or two countries or from the earth to the moon.

Let's see how we can use the new METRIC
SYSTEM.

Kathy can find out the living
room in her house is about
3 meters wide and 5 meters long.

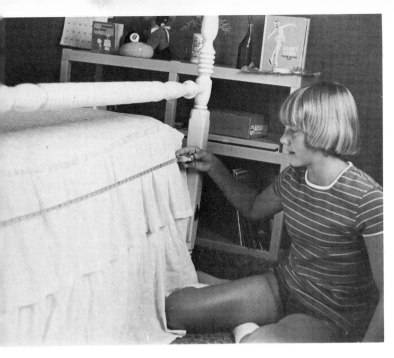

She can find out her bed is about 1 meter wide and 2 meters long.

George and his friend measured their garden and found out it was 5 meters by 7 meters.

Soccer players use a field that is about 110 meters long and about 68 meters wide.

A dime is about 1 millimeter thick.

This book is almost 20 centimeters wide.

A dollar bill is a little more than 15 centimeters wide and 6 centimeters high.

The newspaper in your town is probably about 60 centimeters long and 35 centimeters wide.

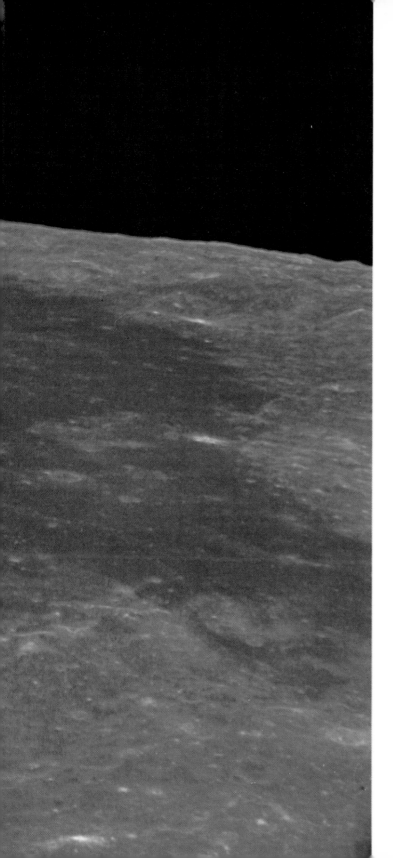

Scientists have found the average distance from the earth to the moon is 384 403 kilometers.

This downtown street is being widened from 12 meters to 16 meters.

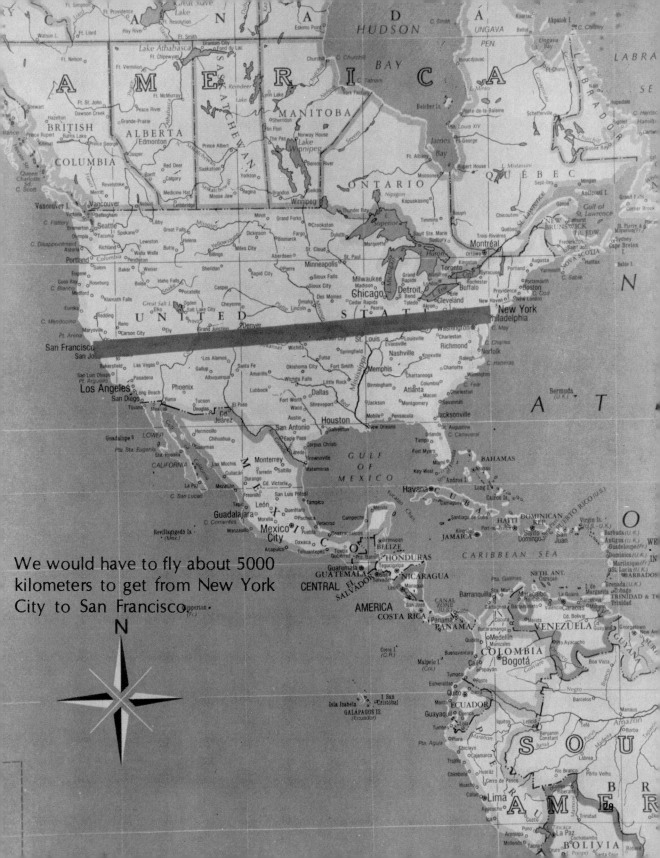

We would have to fly about 5000 kilometers to get from New York City to San Francisco

There is a shorter way to write the units of measurement you learned in this book. They are called symbols.

The symbols for the units of measure for length are:

millimeter	-	mm
centimeter	-	cm
decimeter	-	dm
meter	-	m
dekameter	-	dam
hectometer	-	hm
kilometer	-	km

Try measuring things around your house, your school and your city with THE METRIC SYSTEM.

Now that you know about

the meter

you should meet the rest of
the Metric family.

the metric system is

the liter is

the gram is

the celsius thermometer is

from